Speed-reading

The Comprehensive Guide To Speed-reading – Increase Your Reading Speed By 300% In Less Than 24 Hours

TABLE OF CONTENTS

INTRODUCTION

It has been said that haste makes waste. If you consider the popularity of Aesop's *The Hare and the Tortoise* fable, you'd quickly get the impression that doing things fast isn't wise, but that's not necessarily the case.

In today's day and age, productivity is the holy grail of just about everything from personal activities to business ones. But what is productivity? It simply means getting as many things done as best as they can be done and as quickly as they can be done. In fact, given two activities or processes of equal quality, the one that's faster wins the competition hands down.

What lends credibility to the earlier saying and the fable is speed for speed's sake and at the cost of quality. Indeed, haste can indeed make waste when quality is sacrificed. Speed with quality, however, is a very valuable commodity.

When it comes to reading, speed is of the utmost importance. Your ability to read and comprehend rapidly can spell the difference between good grades and excellent ones, between a mediocre self-published book and a best-selling one and between a so-so business presentation and one that commands a standing ovation, among many other important things. This e-book is about helping you read much faster than you do now.

In Chapter 1, you'll gain a better appreciation for the art of reading, as well as for speed-reading, when to use speed-reading and the common obstacles to it. In Chapter 2, you'll learn to prepare well before learning to read fast so that you'll be able to master speed-reading. In Chapter 3, you'll find out the best speed-reading techniques, and in Chapter 4, you'll learn the best exercises to help you make the techniques as natural as breathing. Next, you'll continue to learn how to supplement these techniques with non-reading approaches such as optimizing your environment for speed-reading, getting enough quality sleep, eating the right foods, getting enough exercise, using meditation to enhance your ability to focus well, and more!

If you're ready to learn speed-reading, turn the page and let's go.

CHAPTER 1

SPEED-READING 101

" **S**urviving and thriving as a professional today demands two new approaches to the written word. First, it requires a new approach to orchestrating information, by skillfully choosing what to read and what to ignore. Second, it requires a new approach to integrating information, by reading faster and with greater comprehension." – Jimmy Calano

Success requires wisdom, which is the effective application of knowledge. We can't be wise if we don't know. Our ability to gain knowledge of important and relevant things is key to becoming wise. It's like making a delicious cake. Even if we have the ingredients on hand, we can't make it if we don't know *how* to make it.

Information Overload

Never before has there been a time where knowledge is as easy to access as it is now. With the rapid development of the Internet, knowledge has become both such a precious commodity and a very abundant one. With such abundance, however, come issues with accuracy. As the Internet has made it easy for anyone who's adept at browsing the web to become an "expert," sifting the knowledge wheat from chaff has become excruciatingly more challenging.

That's not an excuse for failure, however. It's simply a great challenge to be able to cover as much material as possible, understand that material well and make informed decisions on such materials. It's not a challenge that, quite honestly, we can choose to ignore or decline – unless we don't want to succeed in our current fields of education or occupation.

Speed-reading is the one of the best approaches to successfully take on this challenge. Of all the important free resources available to us, time is the most limited. Rich, poor, educated, illiterate, healthy or unhealthy ... all of us only have 24 hours every day, which makes doing things fast all the more important. To the extent we can read fast is the extent to which we can cover more reading materials and information. This allows us to be able to sift more chaff from the knowledge wheat and, in the process, get more wheat.

Common Obstacles to Speed-Reading

Just like accelerating on a bike or in a car, it's important to have little or no obstacles that can break or prevent momentum build-up when it comes to speed-reading.

From the time that we learned to read for the first time, we developed many habits that are still with us. These habits are what cause us to read slowly and spend an eternity finishing up a single book.

Consider these three to be your speed-reading bumps that you'll need to avoid:

1. Word Fixation: When we read, our eyes normally stop on each word. We call this fixation. Stopping at every word in the text that we're reading slows down our reading and, to a great extent, affects our ability to understand the text well. Why? In terms of speed, consider a 500-word text, with each fixation lasting 1 second. If we stop to read every word, it'll take us 500 seconds or roughly 8 minutes to finish the text. In contrast, if our eyes stop to read words in bunches of, say, 3 per fixation, then we'll be able to read the 500-word text in less than 3 minutes. The fewer the fixations or stops, the faster we can read.

   In terms of comprehension, more fixations can mean slower or less understanding of the text. Why? Ideas are made up of words and not a single word only. As such, ideas are best understood within the context of a group of words. Take, for a basic example, the words, "I, am, very, handsome and yeah." Isn't it easier to just read, "I am very handsome, yeah!" instead of each individual word?

2. Retreating: By this, we mean to say looking back or retracing what we have just read unnecessarily or excessively. Sure, there are quite a few moments when we

need to go back to what we just read, especially if it's quite technical or difficult to understand, but if we do it for just about all that we read in a text, it'll greatly slow down our ability to read and comprehend the materials on hand.

3. The Voice: No, we aren't talking about Adam Levine, Blake Shelton, Christina Aguilera and Cee Lo Green collectively. We're talking about that voice we hear inside our heads when we read texts. Yes, that voice is ours! Reading with our voices in our heads speaking the texts is also known as sub-vocalization.

   How does it slow down our reading? Visual reading is much faster than audible reading, even when reading silently. When we read and imagine ourselves pronouncing the words, we are limited to the speed of audible reading. We can speak 150-200 words per minute, while on average; we can read about 300 to 400 words per minute without saying them in our heads.

More Than Just Speed ... Comprehension

As with reckless driving, excessive speed-reading can prove to be counterproductive. Why? Let's face it, there's a speed limit after which our ability to comprehend what we're reading starts to decline. The whole point of increasing reading speed is to be able to learn faster but not learn less.

Reading isn't worth a dime without comprehension, and comprehension of a written text isn't possible without reading. That's why, when it comes to speed-reading, we'll let comprehension be our safety mechanism. To this extent, the most important gauge of reading speed isn't just the actual words-per-minute or WPM but the effective words-per-minute or EWPM. Excessive speed kills, but the right speed brings life.

CHAPTER 2

GET READY ... GET SET ...

"If you fail to plan, you're planning to fail." – Benjamin Franklin

Consistent with any meaningful and worthwhile improvement program, preparation is key to success. Preparation helps you make the most of your time and resources and allows you to speed up your success. To improve your reading speed, the first preparation step is assessment.

Assessing Current Reading Speeds

I see many similarities between two of my favorite hobbies: reading and running. Even when I first started running, I already had a goal in mind, which was to be able to run straight through for 1 kilometer without stopping. I was able to set that goal because I knew for a fact that I couldn't run straight for more than 100 meters at that time. With an accurate assessment came the ability to set a realistic goal.

How did I measure my straight running distance at the beginning? I used my car's odometer. I started running from a specific location in our subdivision and marked the point at which I was too exhausted to continue. I reset my car's odometer reading and drove from the first to the second point and noted the odometer reading. I also noted where the 1-kilometer point was so that I'd know when I had already achieved my immediate goal of being able to run straight with no walk-breaks for at least 1 kilometer. As I increased my running distance, I switched to a GPS device to accurately measure my runs. Being able to correctly assess my runs allowed me to accurately gauge any progress or digress. I am now able to run 10 kilometers easily without stopping.

It's the same with reading speed. It'll be hard to know if the exercises and techniques you'll learn here are already working for you, which can either discourage you from continuing or bore you to quit abruptly. When you're able to objectively see your progress, you'll be invigorated to continue and before you know it, you'll have advanced so far that you won't be able to imagine what you were like at the starting line.

As I mentioned briefly in the previous chapter, we can objectively measure our reading speed in terms of actual words-per-minute (WPM) and effective words-per-minute (EWPM). WPM tells us how fast we read but EWPM tells us how fast we can read with comprehension.

Respectable WPM and EWPM tests can effortlessly be found online through your search engine. Test a trial that measures WPM and then try out reading comprehension tests designed to measure EWPM. One of the beautiful things about these online tests is that you don't have to think about timing yourself and can focus entirely on reading and comprehending the material.

After four weeks of applying the techniques and doing the exercises that will be taught later, test yourself again to see your progress. I highly recommend you do take these tests for your sake. When you see objective progress on your performance, you'll want to continue applying the techniques and applying the exercises to improve even further.

Goal Setting

As with running and any other worthwhile endeavor, you'll need to have a goal. Why? Without goals, speed-reading will just be trivial and will eventually become a meaningless pursuit at worst and a vague endeavor at best. When this happens, you'll lose the drive to develop speed-reading skills and eventually drop it without realizing your true reading potential.

So what kind of goal should you set for speed-reading? First, it should be realistic. If your current reading speed is only 200 words-per-minute and you set a goal of reading 1,000 words-per-minute within one week, you're only setting yourself up for failure because the odds of being able to improve by that much in such a short span of time are not in your favor.

A 25% increase in both WPM and EWPM within a week is more realistic, which can help you improve your reading speed by 300% in 12 weeks. With smaller and more achievable milestones, you're encouraged to continue and succeed. In stating this, however, please note there have been countless cases of people who, through applying these techniques, have actually been able to increase their reading speeds by three-fold in less than 24 hours, although it's not typical.

I can't overemphasize the importance of setting a time limit for accomplishing your speed-reading goals. Without a definite deadline, you may be tempted to procrastinate and increase your risk of quitting. Consider Parkinson's Law when you set a timetable for your speed-reading goals. Parkinson's Law states that a task's perceived importance increases as the time allotted for it decreases. This explains why most people like to cram ... and do a very good job at it!

Your Reading Plan

Although applying the exercises and techniques in this e-book will help you read 300% faster, the value of preparing before reading a text shouldn't be underestimated. A good reading plan can supplement speed-reading techniques and maximize results.

The first part of your reading plan is purpose. Why are you reading the text and what do you hope to get out of it? Do you simply want to get key facts and figures or do you want to understand a process that's discussed in it? By knowing your purpose for reading a text, you'll be able to read faster and with more comprehension.

What are the common purposes for reading texts? These are:

- To thoroughly understand;

- To get a general overview of a text;

- To acquire supporting information for an argument;

- To know the next steps or events;

- To answer a specific question;

- To get an idea of how people perceive a specific topic; and

- To get accurate figures and facts.

The second part of a good reading plan is choosing the relevant materials for the identified purpose. This helps you speed up reading and comprehension by eliminating materials that will only waste your time and effort. By limiting your reading materials to only those that are relevant, you can greatly speed up both reading and comprehension of a certain topic.

CHAPTER 3

SPEED-READING TECHNIQUES

Running fast isn't just a matter of going at it full speed. The fastest human beings in the world combine both power and technique because without technique, power can't be maximized and without power, technique can't be exploited.

In this chapter, we'll look at speed-reading techniques that will help you become more efficient and raise your reading pace significantly for the same effort.

Reading the Table Of Contents

Did you know that there is an enormous speed increase when reading if one knows the general gist of what's being talked about? Did you know that, in addition to reading faster, one could also comprehend much more as well through this method?

How can somebody have a grip on the whole book within a few minutes? That's right, you've guessed it, it's as simple as reading the table of contents. Almost all books have been outlined in this section, and if you read them and form an idea of what the book is about, it'll make it that much faster in reading and comprehending.

Let's use Shakespearean plays as an example. To the average person, reading Shakespeare plays can be difficult because the English used differs from modern English in many respects, which we won't go into detail here. If before reading the play, one were to have a minor grasp of the outline of the play, the characters, plot, story, etc. it would be much faster and easier in both reading and comprehending because you wouldn't stop at trivial parts and, also, complex parts would come to you easier. The same thing happens when reading books in general; the more understanding you have of what's going to be talked about, the faster you'll read it.

Note – Don't use this technique for books that you desire to appreciate like great fiction books, otherwise you'd be spoiling yourself of a brilliant story.

Asking Questions

Another method at your disposal to escalate your reading speed considerably is through asking yourself well-defined questions about the book; this will aid your mind in getting a firm grasp of the ideas about to be presented. The trick to this approach is to grab a sheet of paper and a pencil and jot down questions regarding the book. Go over carefully all the topics and sub-topics then write questions on your paper such as ...

1. What is the main idea in this chapter about?

2. What does the author wish to convey in this particular sub-topic?

3. What is this book about?

4. What is the author wishing to convey through this book?

5. How can I benefit from this book?

You get the idea. When asking yourself these questions, it's recommended to shut the book and keep your mind locked onto the written questions then jot down your answers.

When done, read the chapter. You'll find that your mind will be thoroughly locked onto the information at hand and you'll burn through the text that much faster. You'll also become adept in entirely skipping the fluff in books because, generally speaking, there is TONS of filler text in books. By knowing what's essential and what's not, you can easily ignore material that doesn't contribute much to the main idea and, thus, spend less time reading.

Meta-Guiding

As children, we were taught the practices of using our fingers to run below the text while reading it. This is meant to help us read faster and also avoid sub-vocalization. As you know, sub-vocalization stands for repeating the words in your mind or by moving your lips. This wastes your time and effort. So the best thing to do is do away with this habit altogether.

This method of running your fingers beneath the text is known as Meta-Guiding. Although it seems extremely rudimentary and straightforward, you'll be pleasantly surprised at just how considerably your reading speed can improve when using this technique.

There are different ways of doing this. One way, for example, is you can begin at your handed-side, meaning at the right-most end if you're right-handed and the left-most end if you're a lefty. Put your index finger on the end of the text line according to your hand orientation. From the left side of the line, move your eyes to the right, move your index finger down to the next line and start from the left side again until you finish the last line on the page. Do this at a speed that's comfortable to you at the beginning, then gradually increase your speed by moving your eyes to the right faster, while moving your finger down to the next line faster or both.

Why is Meta-Guiding an effective technique to develop faster reading speeds? It trains your eyes through motion detection, which is what our eyes automatically do to target moving objects, as applied to reading. As you master this technique, you'll come to a point where you will no longer need to use a finger because your eyes have already adjusted to doing it automatically.

Meta-Guiding is a comparatively easy method of speed-reading. You can easily slide into the habit without much effort. Here are some tips for you to get started on the technique.

The very first thing you need to do is, wrap your mind around the fact that you will be using your finger to place under the text.

Some will think of this as a very childish behavior, but it will go a long way in helping you read fast. Most people prefer to use their pointing finger, but you can use whichever finger feels comfortable.

If you don't wish to use your fingers, then you can also use a handy ruler. Place the ruler below the text and start reading. The ruler can be small and fit right into your pocket.

Some people also make use of a piece of thread to serve the purpose. They will place one end of the thread at one end of the sentence and the other end at the other end of the sentence and start reading.

The main aim here is to increase your words-per-minute. So try reading as fast as you can to understand the text efficiently.

When you develop the confidence with time, then you can stop using your finger to place below the text. At this point, it'll become easy to quickly read everything just by running your eyes over the text.

Advantages of Meta-Guiding

The main advantage of Meta-Guiding is that you can read a lot of complex text within a short period of time. You can swiftly run your fingers or ruler below the text and read the data.

The second advantage of this technique is that you can eliminate sub-vocalization. As you know, indulging in sub-vocalization slows you down considerably. Your brain is not capable enough of doing two complex tasks at once. By making use of the Meta-Guiding technique, you can eliminate your habit of sub-vocalization.

Disadvantages of Meta-Guiding

The disadvantage of Meta-Guiding is developing the habit of running your finger under the words too quickly without comprehending the material; it's important to first begin at a pace suitable for your level, and finding this balance would be key.

Another disadvantage is keeping this habit when you're proficient to the point where you don't need it anymore. You might end up hindering your speed when you no longer require it but are still using it.

If you are already of the habit of running your fingers under the text, then try increasing the pace.

Visualization

One important aspect of speed-reading is visualization. Visualization refers to making mental images of the texts. When you create these mental images, you can remember the text better and for longer periods of time, which will help you read faster; just ponder, some long novels which can take a month to read can be viewed within a three-hour movie. You must further enhance this quality by trying to create vivid images in your mind whenever you read. Your mind should literally paint images of whatever you read in full HD.

Keyword Search

Keywords aren't just for search engine optimization or SEO — they're also important for speed-reading. Remember how it's considered a no-no to read texts word-for-word, particularly if speed-reading's the goal? Looking for keywords can be a great way to speed up your reading. But why?

Whether you like it or not, there are countless critical words we don't understand, chiefly when reading upon topics which are foreign to us. In these cases, it's vital that we do a careful keyword search before continuing the task of speed-reading. Examples of keywords you'll need to take earnestly are words that you're unfamiliar with. It will hardly do you any good to speed through text that contains abundant words you don't understand, particularly if it's a topic with many industry-specific terminologies. Do a quick search of these words and understand them; this will help tremendously in the long run.

Keyword searching is a great technique to help you read faster because it can help train your mind to focus on what's important and is more efficient in spotting words that can slow you down while reading. It also helps by limiting the tendency to subvocalize while reading and by widening your peripheral vision to reduce the number of fixations.

Chunk Reading

Chunk reading – also known as chunking – is a reading technique wherein you group together words in a way that forms an idea. Remember that we don't read and comprehend on a word-for-word basis and that doing so drastically slows our reading down? Reading the words together as a coherent unit makes for faster reading and better comprehension.

Although it sounds as if chunking should come naturally to you, your general orientation as a child can make it quite a challenge at first. It's because when you were first learning to read, your teacher taught you to read on a word-for-word basis. And rightly so! You needed to get the ideas and meaning behind the words first. Unfortunately, some childhood orientations were left untouched while growing up, and reading on a word-for-word basis is one of them.

An example of chunking – indicated by "/" – is this:

> "After going out of the house/, I noticed something very odd/: The mail wasn't in the mailbox/, it was outside the door/. I felt nervous/ thinking the mailman went inside the compound/ and didn't ask permission to do so/."

When it comes to chunking, the important thing to consider isn't the size of the "chunk" but that it is able to convey the idea to you. So don't follow others' chunking size or pattern – follow one that makes the text understandable to you. Just don't make the chunk so big that it takes up a whole paragraph! Chunk in such a way that the idea is clear with as few words as possible. To get better at this technique, you'll need to expand your peripheral reading vision using the exercises in the next chapter.

Skim 'N Scan

Skimming

Skimming, as the name suggests, deals with skimming through a text. As you know, skimming refers to removing the top layer of cream that forms on hot milk. Similarly, the central idea of the text is extracted through skimming.

Skimming is a very useful speed-reading technique and one that can be performed easily. All you have to do is read the first and last paragraph of the text and also read the first lines of each paragraph. Most of the key information will be centered on these areas. Once you read these, you will know what the basic message is and you won't have to go through the entire text.

Skimming pays attention to the "speed" bit of speed-reading, so it capitalizes on your speed-reading efficiency and how fast you can read the gist of the paragraph.

This speed-reading technique is widely used for its practical application. Imagine having to go through a large text within a short period of time; you will have to put in a lot of time and effort in doing so. But if you choose this technique, then you can finish reading in no time at all.

But there are some things that you must consider when you wish to adopt this technique.

The very first thing to consider is that the skimming technique must only be used when you wish to understand just the gist of something and not the whole thing. In short, you will not be able to understand the finer details present in the text and will only have the chance to take in the central theme.

This technique is best preferred when you wish to skim through important texts before giving it a full read. Now you may wonder as to why you have to read the same text twice, especially if you are trying to speed-read. The answer is, if you skim first, the data present in the text will fall into place easily in your mind when you do tackle it more fully. You will know exactly what is coming up next and won't waste time trying to understand it. For example, the first line of the book says, "There was a man named Tom." The first line of the second paragraph says, "He invented Velcro." The first line of the third paragraph will read, "The invention gained immense popularity in Europe." Now, you know exactly how the passages are placed, and the flow of the text will become predictable.

Here too, you need to exercise some of your reading skills. You must be alert while reading and know where to jump after you are done reading a line.

Let us look at some tips that will allow you to skim through material with ease:

1. The first thing to do is size up the text. Look at how long it is and estimate the number of words that might be present in it.

2. The second thing to do is understand whether it is the first time that you are reading the text or if it is something very familiar. Many times, we would have forgotten about something that we have already read or know. So see if you can identify some of the things in the text.

3. The third thing to notice is whether the text is real or fictitious. This technique will not suit the latter as much as it will the former.

Advantages of skimming

The main advantage of skimming is that it is easier to finish reading a big text in express time. This is extremely useful if you have an important exam approaching and you haven't started studying yet. If you skim through it and understand the central theme, you can easily understand the basics and then fill in the rest of the data through your smarts. However, don't rely on this technique for every exam you study for; this should be reserved as an emergency technique.

Disadvantages of skimming

The main disadvantage of skimming is that people fail to understand what it actually means. They assume that it refers to reading a few random sentences in the text and understanding it. But that, in no form, is skimming. You cannot randomly land on a page and start reading. There needs to be a structure to it. You must understand that the first and last paragraphs are to be compulsorily read and apart from the first lines of each paragraph; you can also read the last lines. Doing so will give you a fair idea of what the text contains.

All things considered, skimming is a great technique to employ if you have to read the details of an agreement form. By reading the first lines of each paragraph, you can understand what the form is trying to convey to you. You don't have to waste your time understanding the different explanations that are provided for each and every subsequent point mentioned in the form and thus you are able to save an abundant amount of time.

Scanning

Scanning is a technique that is preferred next to skimming. We all know what a scanner is and how it functions. Similarly, you are required to scan through a text quickly.

It is a little similar to skimming in that it allows you to skim through the text but not in detail. You will have to read through it and fish out the important data present in it. So, you will only be looking for whatever you need to know and skip going through the rest of it.

This technique is best if you wish to extract some key elements from the text like names or numbers. You can easily do so by scanning the text once.

Here are some things to consider when you wish to make use of this technique:

1. The first thing to understand is what exactly you seek to find from your text, whether it is a set of names, or numbers or any information that is hidden in the text.

2. The next thing to look for is the flow of the data in the text. Read the first paragraph and see where the information is present in it. The rest of the paragraphs will be most likely structured the same way.

3. The third thing to assess is whether you already know where the data that you are looking for is present on the page. You might know where to look instantly and be done with your scanning in no time.

Once you answer all these questions successfully, you can start scanning the text.

Advantages of scanning

The main advantage of scanning is that it becomes quite easy for you to look for small data that is scattered in the text. You don't have to read the entire thing and waste your time. As soon as you are done collecting the data, you can move to other tasks.

Another advantage is that, while you scan for the important information, you will also get to read snippets of other information present on the page. This means you can avail some extra information apart from what you are particularly looking for.

Disadvantages of scanning

The main disadvantage of scanning is that it is a superficial form of reading. If you are looking for names hidden in a text, then what if you end up picking up the wrong names? So, to help solve this issue, you must evidently also read the sentence where the name is present on the text. That will ensure that you pick up the correct data.

Another disadvantage is that you might have to read the entire thing if the information that you are looking for is scattered here and there. You will end up wasting time and energy in doing so.

All said and done, scanning remains one of the most preferred speed-reading techniques in the world. In fact, I'm sure you are already using this technique in your day-to-day life. All you have to do is practice it the right way and use it to your advantage.

Skimming works best when reading non-fiction material. There are several ways to skim a piece of reading material:

- Title;

- Main Headings;

- Sub-Headings;

- Table of Contents or Indexes;

- Words in Bold Letters;

- Bullet Lists;

- The Back Cover (physical books); or

- -Summaries and Reviews.

Although different, scanning and skimming are two popular speed-reading techniques that are often confused for each other. When you scan a piece of material, you have a target in mind. When you skim through that material, you're looking for meaningful ideas. In scanning, you already know what you're looking for – you already have an idea in mind. Scanning is a great speed-reading technique when you're already familiar with the reading material and you already have an idea of what to look for. With skimming, you don't have an idea yet and that's what you're looking to find in the material.

CHAPTER 4

SPEED-READING EXERCISES

As with sports, techniques are best mastered with technique-specific exercises. In this chapter, you'll learn some of the best speed-reading exercise to help you master the techniques en route to increasing your reading speed by as much as 300%.

Eye Speed

This exercise can help train your eyes to move faster, which obviously translates to faster reading. To do this, move your eyes from numbers 1 to 4 and back to 1 in the picture by following the arrows:

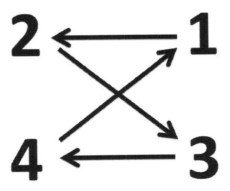

Next move your eyes from 1 to 4 and back to 1 in the picture again by following the arrows:

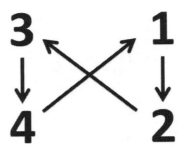

Do each of the exercises 10 times every day but if your eyes feel tired or painful, stop and close them for a few seconds before continuing.

Peripheral Vision Expanders

These exercises can help expand your peripheral vision and help you master the chunking technique. When you do master it, you can reduce your average fixations for faster reading.

Focus on the heart at the middle of the picture and, without removing your sight on it, read all of the letters surrounding it aloud.

Once you're able to read all the letters without removing your eyes from the heart, you can move to the next picture.

And the next ...

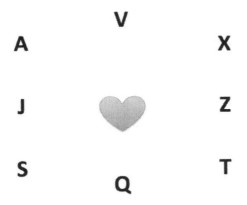

And lastly ...

Now, the next time you are practicing how to speed-read, practice this peripheral vision technique. Stop fixating on each word and practice using your peripheral to help you read chunks of words at a time. This one trick alone can increase your reading speed by 300%. Just like any other skill, it may be a bit uncomfortable at first because you're not used to it but, with practice, you'll get better in no time.

Speed-Reading Exercises for Eyes

Your eye movements are controlled by muscles in your eyeballs and eye sockets and, like your other body muscles, you can also strengthen them through exercise. Here are some major speed-reading exercises for the eyes.

Thumb-To-Thumb Glancing

This exercise stretches the eye muscles to make them more flexible and healthier, as well as moves the muscles in your eye sockets that are responsible for controlling peripheral vision. Try to glance at your thumbs without moving your head if you want to get the most from this exercise:

- Standing or sitting, look straight ahead, stick up your thumbs, after stretching your arms out to your sides.

- Glance back and forth between your right and left thumbs 10 times without turning your head.

- Repeat both of the steps three times.

Eye Writing

Eye writing gets you to move your eyes in such ways that are not related to normal seeing. This gives your eyes a good workout. Eye writing works out the muscles of the eye socket and is particularly good for increasing the flexibility of the eyeball and range of motion. You just need to follow a few steps for the eye writing exercise:

- Look at the wall that is farthest away from you or in another room.

- Now imagine that you're writing your name with your eyes on the wall.

- In simple words, you just need to move your eyes as you would move a pointer if you were writing the letters of your name on the wall.

Hooded Eyes

This exercise helps in relaxing your eyes. You have to do this exercise 2-3 times when your eyes want a quick timeout.

- First of all, close your eyes partially and focus to stop your eyelids from shivering.

- As you focus on your eyelids, you are actually soothing your eyes.

- Look at an object that is far from you, with your eyes still closed partially.

- Your eyes will stop shivering.

Eye Squeezes

This exercise is another good way to relax your eyes that helps in increasing the flow of oxygen and blood to your face and eyes. This exercise will only take three minutes:

- As you inhale slowly and deeply, open your mouth and eyes as wide as you can and at the same time stretch out all the muscles of your face.

- When you exhale, squeeze your closed eyes as tightly as you can and also squeeze all the muscles of your head, face, and neck at the same time and clench your jaw.

- Hold your breath and continue to squeeze for half a minute.

- Repeat all the above steps at least 4 times. Now take a short break, and then do another set of 4-5 squeezes.

Exercises to Increase Your Comprehension

Comprehension is defined as the ability to understand the meaning of something. Reading is one of the most complex things humans can do. Reading is actually a process that requires you to recognize a set of symbols or a symbol, forming a pattern that connects to another set of meanings stored and learned previously in the mind.

Literacy requires you to understand the symbol, as well as the underlying meaning behind those symbols. Comprehension is vital to the social and mental standing of an individual. The increase in comprehension acts as a force multiplier because, the more a person is able to comprehend with the least amount of input and time, the greater the benefit. Even a minor edge in comprehension can make an important difference with time.

Speed-reading is a good way to learn more in less time; however, some studies show that when a person is skilled in speed-reading, he can read up to 1,000 words per minute. However, the reader's comprehension rate is at 50 percent, which is not at all acceptable for the development of better comprehension. Here are a few tips that can help you to achieve the desired level of comprehension, along with speed-reading.

- **Practice self-assessment**

You need to test the level of your comprehension by summarizing the material you just read. If you are able to easily explain the concept in your own words, this means you have understood the subject matter completely. This gets easier as time passes.

- **Push the limits of comprehension**

You can test and measure your level of comprehension through questionnaires. This includes connecting the dots, crossword puzzles, etc. The best thing about this exercise is that you can do this in the comfort of your own home without assistance.

- **Enhance Meta Cognition**

Meta Cognition is actually the ability to "think about thinking." This is used as a tool to catch your thoughts that are not practical and logical. This exercise detaches a person from his own thoughts to check if they are biased.

- **Open your mind**

You need to read extensively. Comprehension is only possible through extensive learning. When you are reading a lot about various subjects, this increases your comprehension speed because you gain the ability to spot differences and similarities.

- **Communicate**

Take out time to speak with people of various socioeconomic and cultural backgrounds. Every person has a different opinion and, while you may or may not agree with their opinions, there is always something that you can learn from their points of view.

- **Contemplate**

It is also important to spend some time reflecting on what you just read, and turn the ideas inside out and upside down in your mind.

Other Speed-Reading Exercises

Here are a few interesting and important speed-reading exercises designed to help you boost your speed-reading skills: reading aggressively, expanding your vision span, avoiding vocalizing, and concentrating harder.

- ✓ **Push-down exercises**: In this exercise, you have to read the same material several times, reading the same amount of material in less time each go-around. You also have to answer when, where, what, and who questions, as this will demonstrate how recall, retention, and compre-hension improve after each reading.

- ✓ **Push-up exercises:** In this technique, you read the same material several times for the same amount of time.

However, try your best to read farther and farther in that allotted time each go-around. Push-up exercise shows your familiarity with vocabulary and text and also increases reading speed.

Both push-up and push-down exercises really challenge you to bear down and apply all your speed-reading skills. Moreover, they give you an opportunity to realistically measure how much faster you can read if you put your mind and heart into it.

✓ Alarm Clock Reading Exercise

1. Select an interesting book or novel and keep it for the purpose of speed-reading exercise only.

2. Set the timer to go off after 20 minutes of reading.

3. Now read the subject matter as rapidly as possible until the timer stops.

4. After this, note the number of pages you have read in this time.

5. Next step is to paraphrase out loud the material you just read.

6. At the next reading, try to read faster in order to break the habit of plodding and slow reading on easy material.

You need to do this exercise daily and keep your record up to date to check your progress. Try your best to read a few more lines each time.

Timed Reading Exercises

The best way to perfect your reading speed skills is to practice, practice, practice, and that's what 'timed reading exercises' are all about.

- **One-Minute Timing Exercise**

This exercise is an easy and quick way to see how you interact with your speed strategies. Here's what you need to do:

1. Choose an article to read silently for exactly one minute.

2. At the end of one minute, just mark the line you're on.

3. Now write down as many important points as you can remember on a separate piece of paper without looking back at the reading.

4. Calculate your WPM.

5. WPM = # of lines read × number of words per line

6. Now determine your comprehension percentage of how much you think you understood based on the main points you wrote down. Make a chart and record your results daily.

- **3-2-1 Drill Exercise**

This exercise is a great way to learn about how to break out of your slow reading habits.

1. Choose an article to read silently for exactly one minute.

2. At the end of one minute, just mark the line you're on.

3. Now write down as many important points as you can remember on a separate piece of paper without looking back at the reading.

4. Now go back and reread the same text. However, this time, give yourself two minutes to reach the same point. At the end of two minutes, you can add more important points to your comprehension sheet.

5. After this, again go back to where you first began and read for just one minute, stopping at your original three-minute ending point. At the end of three minutes, you can add more important points to your comprehension sheet.

6. Make a chart and record your results daily.

Chunks Reading Exercise

This exercise involves skipping individual, single-word reading in favor of lessening the number of "stops" that your eyes perform as you read and processing larger groupings of words.

This exercise leads to an increase in the comprehension of compound ideas, and hence, helps you to be able to understand the meaning of what you are reading with greater speed.

Take a look at the following paragraph to practice chunks. The following paragraph is separated into chunks using slash marks. You have to read and digest each slash mark as quickly as you can and then move on to the next. After this, feel how your eyes like to move ahead.

Paragraph:

If you are really thinking/about getting your money/under control,/then it is important/to first analyze/your habits of spending./ Begin by reviewing/your register of checkbook./ Then for 4 weeks,/note down everything/you use money on,/from the fast food meals /to coffee lattes /to other necessities./ After the month,/ check/and add up/your everyday expenditures./ You might be surprised/at the amount you spent./ Learn from this/ and then make necessary adjustments./

Speed Reading Comprehension Test

You need to follow the below steps to take your comprehension speed-reading test. This test will help in determining your both comprehension as well as reading speed.

Instruction:
- Using a stopwatch, clock or watch, note what time you start reading.

- Read the following passage at your fastest speed with the most comfortable understanding rate.

- Finally, answer all the comprehension questions and note how many questions you got correct.

- Determine your WPM rate and comprehension speed rate by following mathematical rules.

1. Calculate your WPM.

WPM = # of lines read × number of words per line = ____

2. Calculate Your Comprehension %.

Number of correct answers / Total number of questions x100 = ____

Passage:

In the new knowledge economy, reading is becoming more and more important and remains the most effective activity for humans to transform information into knowledge.

The top readers generally read at speeds of above 1,000 wpm with around 85% comprehension; however, they represent just 1% of readers. The majority are average readers with just 200 wpm and a comprehension rate of 60 percent.

This means that the average reader is 5 times slower than the top reader. Things are even worse if we consider both reading speed as well as efficiency.

Every computer user who also has a slow typing speed is aware of the advantages he could gain with a typing course; however, nearly no one suspects the much higher gains he could reach by enhancing his reading speed and comprehension. The rapid enhancement of voice recognition may slowly make typing obsolete since a typist performs well under the speed of speech. But, on the other hand, computer or human speaking, with an average speed of 150 wpm, will always remain much slower than a good reader.

There are three major ways to improve reading. Probably the fastest is a speed-reading seminar animated by a dynamic instructor and based on good materials. However, when this encouraging and rapid improvement is not sufficiently anchored, it usually fades with time.

The second possibility is a book about speed-reading. Such a book generally provides comprehension speed tests as well as tips to improve reading. However, a book-based technique requires a strong commitment from the reader as well a lot of time.

Finally, the most efficient way to achieve top reading levels is a speed-reading computer program. Computers provide unique exercises for boosting reading efficiency through pacing, text animation, and interactivity.

Total Words: 287 Words

Q1. Compared to an average reader, the top reader reads with?

A. Same Reading Comprehension And Higher Speed

B. Better Reading Comprehension And Higher Speed

C. Worse Reading Comprehension And Higher Speed

Q2. Who are the ones who read above 1,000 wpm?

A. The 1 % minority

B. The majority of readers

C. The average readers

Q3. What is the average reading speed?

A. 200 wpm

B. 150 wpm

C. 120 wpm

Q4. What is the average reader comprehension speed?

A. 85%

B. 60%

C. 50%

Q5. Most computer users want to?

A. Purchase a large screen

B. Improve reading skills

C. Improve typing skills

Q6. A book or speed reading seminar lacks?

A. Detailed explanations

B. Consistent practice

C. Rapid results

Q7. What is the best way to get to the top level of reading efficiency?

A. Speed-reading software

B. A speed-reading seminar

C. A speed-reading book

ANSWERS: 1B, 2A, 3A, 4B, 5C, 6B, 7A

CHAPTER 5

SUPPLEMENTAL STRATEGIES

Mastering speed-reading techniques can definitely help you significantly increase your reading speed. However, you can still supplement it with other non-reading strategies to really maximize the speed-reading gains you can get from it.

Reading Environment

Whether you like it or not, where you read plays a very huge role in your ability to read and comprehend materials quickly. With focus being the single most important ingredient for speed-reading success, you'll need to read in a place where there is virtually no distraction whatsoever. If not, at least keep it to a manageable level.

One of the characteristics of a great reading environment is adequate lighting. If the lights are too low, you'll strain your eyes quickly and you'll easily get tired from reading. If the lighting's too soft, it can be too relaxing and make you feel too relaxed to be able to read well. I love reading in a well-lit, quiet coffee shop – those with big windows to allow much sunlight to come in. If you wish to read at night then have a tube light or bulb that is slightly away from your head. If it is directly above you then you will have issues with shadow formation on your book.

You'd also need to avoid places that are too illuminated. Yes, there are places like that, especially if the lights are fluorescent ones. If the lights are too bright, you may also experience reading discomforts like headaches, which can keep you from reading as much as you like.

Another aspect of the ideal environment is silence. The noisier the place where you read is, the more distracting it can be. I love reading at home, especially when everyone is away, because it's so quiet – though I put on some soft jazz music in the background to keep me from being too relaxed. Personally, I don't like to do significant reading in most coffee shops because of the noise, but I do know a few shops that are quiet enough for me to drown in books. But, hey, noise tolerance is subjective, and the important thing is the environment where you plan to read shouldn't be distracting to you alone.

Another important characteristic of the ideal reading environment is that it should offer you enough privacy to read uninterrupted. If you're dead serious about reading uninterrupted, go to a place where it's difficult for people to have access to you. You can have a dedicated reading room in your house if space permits; this is a favorite among many people, as you can customize the room to what suits you the best. After customizing the room, just shut the door behind you, put a DND sign outside, and happy readings.

As a personal tip, to make the room even cozier you can light a few aromatherapy candles if you prefer that. Your mind and body will feel calm and relaxed while you read.

Focus

All the speed-reading techniques in the world won't matter much if you're unable to focus well enough on what you're reading. The ability to focus is partly dependent on environment, but it's also highly dependent on your mind. Sometimes, it can still be hard to focus even in the perfect reading environment, particularly when a lot of things are running through your head. That's why it's important to work on the internal environment as well – the mind.

There are several good ways to help develop mental focus. One is to know the things that you have and don't have control over. Many times, distractions come in the form of worry over pending issues like health, the economy, and even world peace. Many times too, these worries fall outside your circle of influence or control, like the country's economy, price of oil in the international market, random shootings by crazy extremists, and even the highly anticipated "big-one" earthquake. It's easier to let issues like these go when you acknowledge that, really, you can't do anything about them and that you're better off focusing on things that you have direct control of or influence over ... like reading!

Another way is to do yoga or some other meditation exercises. These help train your mind to focus on the present, to be in the moment, so to speak. You see, the mind is a muscle for all intents and purposes. With enough exercise, it becomes stronger. Similarly, when you exercise your mind to focus, it will become stronger at it and will help you reap as many of the speed-reading benefits as possible.

Lastly, I highly recommend a very practical method of focusing that has helped me a lot, not just with reading but in my work as a writer: The Pomodoro Technique. Here, you read uninterrupted for 25 minutes then take a 5-minute break, which constitutes a Pomodoro cycle. When you take a break, you can do something else like walk around or play a game on your smartphone. The point is you rest from the main task at hand, which can be reading.

You'll need to exercise discipline in stopping after 25 minutes and taking a break for 5 minutes no matter how enjoyable your reading material is. The main principle behind this is that by limiting your focus to 25 minutes at the most and taking regular 5-minute breaks, you prevent your mind from tiring out quickly, thus extending your productive and focused time. It's similar to the run-walk-run method for endurance running where you don't wait to be too tired to run before you take a walk break. By resting even before the point of mental fatigue, you extend your ability to focus intensely on the task at hand ... including reading.

Exercise

According to Dr. John Ratey, who wrote the book *Spark – The Revolutionary New Science of Exercise and the Brain*, exercise helps improve your ability to focus for several hours after completion. Exercising a few hours prior to an activity that will require you to focus mentally – like hmmmm ... reading – can help you focus more.

It can also help you with the reading comprehension part of speed-reading by helping you improve your memory through energizing your brain. Speed-reading would be practically a useless endeavor if you didn't retain the important points of what you just read quickly. An experiment published at a well-recognized Sports Medicine University showed that people who are physically more active did better in reading tests compared to those who are less active.

Lastly, regular exercise helps you release pent-up energy that can cause you to be fidgety in situations where you'll need to be still, like reading. Personally, I can attest to the hyperactivity-reducing benefits of regular exercise. When I don't get to run or bike at least three times a week, I find it very hard to concentrate on reading and writing because I feel so agitated and restless. With regular exercise, I'm able to release excess energy and focus much better on things that require focus, such as speed-reading.

Foods – The Bad

Eating the right foods can help you focus much better and retain more of what you read. Nutrients play a vital role in keeping your brain healthy and working optimally and, as such, you'll need to take a serious look at your current diet to see if it's conducive to improving your reading and comprehension.

Let's start with the foods that are bad for mental performance. On top of the list is – surprise – junk food! Why? Well, here are a couple of reasons:

- Hyperactivity: Because many junk foods contain too much sugar, they can make you more hyper than you usually are and prevent you from focusing and concentrating enough on what you're reading.

- Crash and Burn: Again, as many junk foods are very high in sugar, your blood sugar spikes quickly and as your pancreas responds by releasing insulin, your blood sugar crashes as quickly as it spiked. When that happens, you feel a sudden sense of lethargy and drowsiness and WHEN THAT HAPPENS, it'll be very difficult for you to concentrate and focus on what you're reading.

Next on the list of nutritional bad boys when it comes to focus is – surprise again – tuna! Yes, that supposedly heart- and brain-friendly aquatic sea creature can actually wreak havoc on your ability to focus if taken excessively. Eating tuna no more than twice a week is beneficial to your heart and brain, but if you consume it more often you run the risk of ingesting too much mercury, excessive and long-term consumption of which has been scientifically linked to cognitive decline. If you're so into omega-3 fishes, consider healthier alternatives like wild salmon, anchovies, and trout, all of which offer the same brain health benefits without the toxicity.

Another food to minimize, if not avoid altogether, is ice cream. Why? Consider the nutritional value in an average cup of vanilla ice cream: 10 grams of anti-cardio saturated fat and a whopping 28 grams of pure, unadulterated sugar! Several studies have already noted that foods rich in sugar and saturated fat – like your favorite vanilla ice cream – can lead to diminished verbal memory and cognitive performance. If you can't lay off the cold and sweet treats, get Greek yogurt instead and lace it with some brain-friendly berries like strawberries and blueberries to maximize the culinary brain-friendly treat.

Lastly, the seemingly harmless diet soda is another focus- and concentration-killer in sheep's clothing. Why is that so? There's no sugar in those drinks so I'm safe and sound from sugar crashes, right? Right! But that's not why diet sodas are bad for speed-reading and comprehension. The culprit is a controversial sugar substitute called aspartame, which is known to negatively affect memory. What good is speed-reading if you don't remember what you read, right?

Foods – The Good

Now that the bad guys are over and done with, we'll take a look at foods that can boost your ability to focus and concentrate for maximum speed-reading and comprehension.

First on the list – blueberries! Numerous studies have established that blueberries have the uncanny ability to elevate memory and concentration as much as five hours after consumption. The secret lies in their abundant supply of antioxidants, which help promote healthy blood flow to the brain and, as you well know, good blood flow means good performance. Place a bowl of the berries on your dining table or office table and munch some every now and then. You will also remain energetic all through the day when you consume these berries.

Next on our list of nutritional superheroes for focus and concentration is green tea! What makes green tea a great mental boost? Two words: caffeine and l'theanine. I think you already know why caffeine is good for improving focus and mental performance, right? Right! This leaves us with l'theanine. Simply put, l'theanine is an ingredient that, among other things, help release caffeine slowly instead of dumping it all at once, which can lead to what's known as a caffeine crash, i.e., sudden lethargy due to sudden drops in caffeine levels in the blood. L'theanine also can help you feel more tranquil. Tranquil alertness is a very good state to be in when you're speed-reading for comprehension.

As we mentioned earlier, fatty fish like trout and salmon contain omega-3 fatty acids that are crucial for staving off memory decline, fatigue, and mood swings; they've been known to help improve concentration and mood as well. It is best to bake them as opposed to frying them; you can also try lightly roasting them.

There was once a famous violinist who disguised himself and, with a very luxurious violin, performed brilliant compositions to the ears of passing citizens on the streets of Manhattan. This individual was the chief attraction at numerous symphonies that charged hundreds of dollars and yet he was playing for FREE on this particular day. The astounding surprise was that 99.9% of the people passed him by that day without giving a second thought to him. Why? One may ask ... It's because people take free stuff for granted!

Water is one item that's often taken for granted when it comes to consumption and, as such, many people suffer from slight dehydration, which can negatively affect your ability to focus and concentrate. Water provides your brain the necessary electrical energy for optimal functioning including memory and thought activities. It has also been proven that being adequately hydrated helps you focus more, think faster and more clearly than when you're dehydrated. Many people don't drink until they feel thirsty but you must force yourself to drink every now and then because your body actually becomes dehydrated prior to the feeling of thirst.

You can also prepare some fruit-infused water, as it will help you remain hydrated and, at the same time, you can increase your nutrition. Just add a few berries into the water and consume it from time to time. It is recommended that you consume this water when you are learning speed-reading techniques – right now, for example!

Dark chocolates – not the sugar-laden and milky processed ones – contain some caffeine and magnesium, which can help you handle stress better. Dark chocolates also help facilitate the body's release of endorphins and serotonin, all of which can help improve your mood and feelings. Being good for speed-reading doesn't mean the more the merrier though. Keep consumption to small amounts because, as with all good things, too much of it can be detrimental to other aspects of your health.

Apart from these, there are certain natural food supplements that you can consume to the benefit of your brain and thus improve your speed-reading. They are mentioned below:

Ashwagandha: Ashwagandha is a natural herb that is widely used in Asian countries. It is said to improve memory power and increase a person's grasping capacity. You can purchase it in powder or capsule form.

Shankpushpi: Shankpushpi is an Indian herb mentioned in Ayurvedic texts. It is regularly consumed to improve memory and sharpen the mind. In fact, many students consume it just before an exam to improve their mind's power. This is mostly consumed in syrup form and can be bought online.

Gingko: Gingko biloba is an extremely popular herb that is widely used in Chinese medicine. It is said to be extremely potent in increasing a person's mind capacity and brainpower.

Rhodiola: Rhodiola is another root that is great for combating memory loss and improving your mind's capacity. By regularly consuming this supplement, you can improve your mind's capacity to speed-read. You can purchase it in powder or capsule form.

Sage: Sage extracts have been mentioned in European texts to help improve a person's memory power. The herb is extremely powerful and you can add a little of it to your meals on a daily basis. It is also easy to grow it yourself!

Turmeric: Turmeric is another good brain food. It is an Indian herb. All you have to do is add a little to your soups and curries. It is also known to help prevent oxidative damage in the brain and improve your brain's overall health.

Although all of these are safe to consume, but you must consult a physician before consuming any of these.

Sleep

Lastly, all the mental exercises and super foods in the world won't be enough to improve your reading speed and comprehension without getting adequate sleep. Just as your physical muscles need ample time to rest and recuperate, so does your brain. I'll beg off from giving a standard for sleeping hours but here's a good guideline to consider: if you feel lethargic or weak when you wake up in the morning, it's highly possible that you're not getting enough. You should be able to wake up feeling energetic, alert, and refreshed. When you do, you'll be able to concentrate and focus better throughout the day.

More than just the number of hours, the quality of your sleep is also important. You can sleep for 10 hours every night but if your sleep is very shallow, you'll still feel 10 hours isn't enough. On the flip side, if your sleep is very deep, you can have just 6 hours and wake up feeling refreshed, alert, and energetic.

For quality sleep, consider the following practical tips:

i.   Avoid exercising close to bedtime. Doing so increases your body temperature significantly and will make it very hard for you to sleep. If you're going to exercise, make sure it'll end at least three hours prior to hitting the sack so you give your body the chance to cool down and your heart rate to normalize.

ii. Turn your gadgets off at least 30 minutes before sleeping. Exposure to artificial light – those coming from your smartphones and tablets – tend to suppress the release of melatonin, which is an important sleep hormone.

iii. Like exercise, having caffeine too close to bedtime can make you too alert to sleep. Limit your caffeine intake to

3 p.m. at the latest to give your body enough time to flush out the caffeine from your system.

iv. Relax. Trying so hard to sleep when your mind and body are clearly aren't up to it will only make it harder for you to sleep. If you can't sleep, read a really boring book (obviously not this one), count sheep (or any animal you like), or meditate. Just don't exert effort because it will only stimulate your mind even more, making it harder for you to sleep.

v. Try having something aromatic in the room that can help you sleep better; this will help you feel good. Just make sure it is a natural fragrance and not artificial. Rose, sandalwood, and jasmine are great choices for you to try out.

vi. It is ideal to maintain a cool temperature in the room. Countless studies have been done to show that sleeping in a cooler room around 18 degrees Celsius is optimal. Keep a thermometer in your room and try to your best to match what's suggested as optimal.

CHAPTER 6

HISTORY OF SPEED-READING

Reading, as a habit, has existed since time immemorial. The world has progressed for thousands of years and it has all been possible owing to books and other decipherable scripts. Imagine a world without any information being read and shared; it would be absolutely horrible, wouldn't it? Nevertheless, don't worry, such a world does not exist and there are millions of books and texts that you can read and explore. Let us look at the history of speed-reading.

As you now know, not everybody reads at the same pace or with the same techniques. Give a 500-page book to two people and one of them will read it in a week while the other will take a month. This is primarily the result of differences in their reading speeds, techniques used, as well as the amount of time they spend reading.

Did you know that "meta-guiding" as a technique did not exist until the late 1950s? For a respectable, educational purpose, Evelyn Wood was determined to understand why some people could read much faster than others could. She wanted to come up with a feasible method that would allow everybody to read at the same pace, which was fast.

Through several years of research, she was unable to increase her own reading speed and believed that it was impossible to finish a book any faster. However, while on the verge of giving up, she stumbled upon a winning formula. She realized that running her finger below the words made it easy for her to read the data faster and that is how meta-guiding is said to have come about.

John F. Kennedy is said to have been an avid speed-reader. He could read text exceedingly fast and also encouraged others around him to take up speed-reading. Another president, Jimmy Carter, along with his wife Rosalyn, also excelled at speed-reading, and he is said to have introduced a course at the White House which prompted several people to take it up seriously.

Today, there are several speed-reading contests that are held all over the world. These competitions generally require the person to read around 1,000 to 2,000 words within a minute with at least 50% comprehension. There are people who can also read 10,000 words within a minute. But this has come under fire from critics, as they believe reading so fast will not allow the person to remember anything at all, not to mention the pressure that it puts on the brain.

The average reading speed that most people have is said to be approximately 250 words per minute, but this can certainly be changed to a higher number. You need to take up speed-reading determinedly, which will help you increase that number to at least 500 to 600 words per minute.

CHAPTER 7

BENEFITS OF SPEED-READING

Knowledge

When we read, we obviously take in a lot of information. Those who are not well read will not have access to much information on a wide range of different subjects. There is an adage that states, "Knowledge Is Power," and so it becomes all the more important to read as much as possible and diversify one's current awareness. This does not always have to be academic and can also be trivial; it's vital to keep in mind that both are equally important and you must expand your horizons through reading books and other texts on diverse subjects if you wish to increase your knowledge base.

Confidence

Reading well leaves a person with an utmost confidence not easily obtained. If you are in a group where everyone is well read and speaks intelligently while you are the only one that does not do so, then it is important that you read and increase your confidence so that you feel that you fit in. Once you develop knowledge, you will start speaking up and contribute to a conversation more confidently. The basic aim is to contribute constructively and you can easily do so by reading books that will provide you with key information on a plethora of topics.

Freedom

The ability to read, or read fast, will free you from having to rely on others to help you understand something. You will not have to rely on others to tell you what you need to know and can quickly start doing a job by yourself. This freedom can go a long way in ensuring that you don't waste your time and can allow you to quickly move to another important task. It will also prevent you from making errors and will not allow others to take advantage of you.

Security

When you are well read, a sense of security starts to creep in. Apart from confidence, you'll also develop this feeling that you can easily handle anything that is put your way. This enables you to forge ahead with the utmost belief in yourself and will also help you toward establishing financial security. Your knowledge and skills will take you a long way and you just might get a raise as well – all too often owing to your skill. So keep reading and improving your vocabulary and cognition; you will successfully reach new heights by doing so.

Memory

Memory power is a big boon to mankind. Imagine a world where nobody has a good memory; it would be quite irritating. To help you improve your memory, the best thing to do is read as much as possible and, in addition, read on a variety of different subjects. Try reading a language book and learning a new language. Doing such extracurricular studies will strengthen both your short-term and long-term memory. You will remember things better and for longer periods of time. Partake in regular memory contests and you will truly see just what a marked difference your speed-reading skills make for you, in no time at all.

Focus

When it comes to reading, focus is of utmost importance. The average human mind is capable of reading 600 words a minute and yet we manage only a couple of hundred. A wise style to increase reading speed is by increasing your focus and vise-versa; once you earnestly take up speed-reading, your focus will automatically start to improve. You will be able to talk to others from different walks of life as you become more present.

Logic

Logic is a mind activity that attaches feasible reasoning to events and occurrences. This type of logic is extremely important for everybody to possess, as it will save a lot of time in reasoning throughout the day. When you read good books, your mind automatically adapts to logic as the flow of the words starts registering inside your mind. As you start to read more and practice speed-reading techniques, your mind will start to hold more information and process it thoroughly; you will realize that, through this, it will become easier for you to think of things and events through a logical perspective.

Emotions

As we know, most of us are now exposed to a lot of stress, which causes us to feel extremely fatigued. Most of us turn to television to relieve ourselves of this stress, without realizing that it is only worsening it for us. We don't understand that most media sources negatively impact our thinking and slow us down, especially binge-watching television shows. The need of the hour is to indulge in an activity that will effectively curb our stress and improve our mind's health, and that activity is reading. When you learn to speed-read, you will find it increasingly easy to read big books; the feeling of getting lost in epic novels is simply amazing. Hence, you can get lost in novels on a daily basis and kiss your stress goodbye. Once you learn to speed-read, you will not feel like stopping! Trust me, it's that good!

Solutions

All human beings wish to seek solutions to their personal issues. Some wish to find solutions to serious problems and some to petty ones, but the core of the matter is to walk away with the cake, by being the first one to find a feasible solution; this can be made possible by reading in excess. You have to read as much as possible and absorb all information like a sponge, and then the information can be employed to find solutions to issues. The human brain is capable of things that you cannot even imagine and, before you know it, it would have already formulated a feasible solution to the problem lying in front of you.

Invention

Our world has existed for thousands of years, but there are still many discoveries waiting to happen out there. If you are adept at reading fast, then you can read a vast number of books within a short amount of time; the key is to absorb as much information as possible very swiftly. Then, mix and match whatever you read and come up with something new. This new information or logic will help you in more ways than you can shake a stick at, so get reading and discover something new!

These form just the tip of the iceberg for uses of speed-reading. There are countless more of these that you can attain once you pick up this art!

CHAPTER 8

SPEED-READING EXPERIENCE ENHANCERS

During the course of reading this book, you may be wondering how you can make speed-reading relevant to your life and use it to make yourself into a better person. Some of the methods for doing this are included in this chapter and they will take your speed-reading to a whole new level.

Debating

Did you ever think that you would believe in something so much that you would be willing to debate it? Well, in this world where there is so much friction, it's quite possible that you can become an important voice of reason. There are many debating societies and these enrich people's lives because people – just like you – who know something about a subject – get a chance to air their views.

Why is this important?

Sometimes you believe in something and feel that you are doing nothing to change the way that the world perceives things. For example, some topics that you could speed-read and really get something out of include the following aspects of everyday life:

- Ecology
- Wars
- Different approaches to government
- Marriage issues
- Religion and politics
- Earth-friendly innovations

If you are going to speed-read, test how powerful you are by joining a debating society and learn to argue your case. This may not seem important, but it's extremely important because what you are doing is learning logical reasoning based on the material that you read, and that's powerful stuff. If you believe in something, learn about what experts say about it. Follow up your reading with suggested readings on Amazon and other websites, which are great places to find those materials.

For example, if you buy a book on global warming, what other books did readers buy? It's usually shown on the Amazon page, and that's really useful information for the avid reader. You get to know about books that argue the case from different perspectives and that makes you a lot more powerful in the way that you put forward your case. You can use quotes from people to back up your argument. If you don't know where to join a debating society, try Facebook because there are groups there that are looking for people like you – people who are informed and who know what they are talking about based upon what they have read and understood from their reading. That's powerful stuff.

Debating helps your reading experience because you will become so keen to check up on information that you absorb it easily, and it is also an excellent way of getting interested in a particular subject. Half of the trick to speed-reading is actually having topics that you enjoy reading about. If they are topics that you have no interest in, it's like trying to read a newspaper in hieroglyphics! You need that interest to spur you on and, believe me, it really will.

Enjoying Your Internet Experience More

Often when people speed-read, they don't realize the significance of reading on reading devices, and this works every bit as well as reading a book in a traditional format. Use the different techniques outlined in an earlier chapter and try using them on your Kindle or e-Reader for a start. The reason I say this is because if you are accustomed to using the Internet, know that the Internet is known as a place where people have low attention spans. Reading your Kindle and learning to speed-read will really help you to see the screen as a reader instead of merely a website with other things to distract you.

When speed-reading online, you may need to use your finger across the screen, just as the original lady did when she learned to speed-read. This may appear to be silly at first, but TRY IT; you'll soon get accustomed to reading in this manner and can take in a lot of information in a very short space of time. This helps you to research at a much deeper and swifter rate than if you simply read as normal Internet users usually do.

I found that speed-reading for data was very important in my life because, when you are studying, this helps you to take in information much faster than simply browsing the Web. What you first need to learn is which websites give the best information and the least distractions. You need authoritative work, but you also need to read several Web pages before you get an overall view of the topic that allows you an original take. For instance, if you are studying, the last thing that your professor wants to see is regurgitated ideas.

People who use speed-reading effectively take in all the ideas and then come up with an original take on those ideas so that what they write is original and very well-researched indeed. I once had to do this with a paper I wrote on Haiti and what I found, to my dismay, was that much of the information that I was reading was out of date and that, had I written my paper from the first few websites that I had visited, the information would have been terribly out of date as well. Fortunately, I was able to make good use of my speed-reading skills and blazed through many credible websites. This helped me to produce a paper that was not only up to date but which also had extremely valuable information that no one else had thought of.

Speed-reading done for a specific purpose is always more rewarding than doing it for the sake of achieving numbers of pages read or number of words. People who are versed in this art are able to piece things together much more easily and use the information that they glean to help them improve who they are and their attitude toward life.

Following Logical Argument by Understanding

When you are out with people who are well read, you are better able to voice your opinion if you are heavily read and have understood the intricacies of the words that you have digested. Unfortunately, not everyone has an understanding of the words that they intake. Many magazines have quizzes every month that test people on word meanings, and this helps to increase the vocabulary of readers. This is a powerful tool and if you can get your hands on these issues, it's worth investing in it to help you to gain more from your reading experience. It's not enough to simply read. Comprehension of what you read is vital, especially if you want your voice to be heard by others.

In an Islamic State, a girl once had very strong views politically and voiced them to make a vast difference in the way people saw things, and this is something that you are able to do if you up your comprehension by taking tests that help you to establish your understanding of complex vocabulary.

If you can't get ahold of these magazines, don't worry. There are websites that help you to improve your vocabulary and which explain words that you don't understand. I have also found that speed-reading on a Kindle helps with understanding complex words because you have instant access to a tool that will explain any words that you don't understand. Thus, you not only learn to speed-read, you learn to speed-comprehend, and that's when things get really powerful.

I cannot emphasize enough how important it is to get the most out of your speed-reading experience. If you want to increase your understanding of life, you need to know what authors mean within the lines of their vocabulary, in addition to reading them fast, because this improves your level of understanding and is much more meaningful than simply being able to read a set amount of words in a set amount of time.

CHAPTER 9

HOW THE HUMAN MIND WORKS

Before you understand how speed-reading works, you must first know how the human mind works.

As you know, the human brain is capable of multi-tasking several things at once and is also adept at storing a lot of information. Our brains are constantly working and it is no surprise that it is the only organ in the body that remains awake while we sleep.

When we sleep, a natural phenomenon occurs where we visualize people and things; this phenomenon is known as dreaming. When a person dreams, his or her subconscious mind supplies the conscious with images and stories, and these images and stories are then relayed like a movie.

This, you may say, is common knowledge, but what many people don't know is that this is the same phenomenon that occurs inside the mind when you read. That is correct; when you read something, you can see all of it like a movie in your head. I remember reading Laurie Lee's *Cider with Rosie* and seeing all the countryside spread out in front of me; descriptive use of language allows you to do that.

When you read the text, your mind focuses on the characters that are present in the book. If there are no characters and you are reading something seriously, it still starts playing everything out like a movie, but perhaps like a documentary.

Say, for example, you are reading a novel where the protagonist is a tall, fair man with blue eyes and blond hair. Your mind will immediately make a mental picture of such a person and as you read, you will imagine this very person going through the different events that are mentioned in the book. So say this person falls in love with a short girl with raven hair; you will imagine these two characters falling in love.

The characters will be based on what you would have already seen in your life, and your mind will only draw out images that are already present. Consequently, there is nothing new that is being invented in your mind and you are only seeing whatever you have stored in your subconscious.

That is exactly why you will see the same image of an alien even if it appears in different books. Your mind will have a preset template of the alien, which it will supply to your conscious.

Research has shown that the person feels like he or she is part of the story when they read something, so if the story is about a man who climbs Mount Everest, then the person will put himself in the mountaineer's shoes. A vivid imagination will help the person comprehend the story faster.

It is understood that the brain does all of this in microseconds, and before you have the time to think something different from what you read, your mind would have already prepared a movie in your head.

This type of movie will be vivid when someone else reads to you. That is why bedtime stories that are read out loud to children are considered to be good brain activity for them. They will learn to visualize better and when they start to read, they will do so with ease.

Now it is obvious that children will read much more enthusiastically as compared to adults, because they are freshly starting out. So to help children develop a permanent reading habit, it is best to choose an interesting book for them, something that will keep their enthusiasm going.

It is believed that it is possible to increase the white mass in the brain, which is the prefrontal cortex. Your hippocampus will also increase in size and allow you to think better as you read and gain deeper understandings of various topics. There is a set pattern that your mind draws from and you must allow your brain to shoot off of.

It is also possible for you to improve your comprehension by doing the following things:

Learning a new language

You can take up fun activities such as learning a new language to improve your comprehension. Don't stick with the standard European languages; pick an Asian language like Chinese or Hindi. The rationale behind this is you ought try to use a language where the alphabet is different; this will open up your mind to seeing something other than the A, B, Cs and you'll begin to see that the world does not only consist of language which is played out in this limited alphabet.

You will feel happy to add another language to your existing repertoire, and your reading comprehension will also improve considerably.

Play focus games

Playing games that require you to focus will also improve your cognition and memory. Choose a word/number game or something to do with quick calculations and try to play regularly. Have you heard of Free Cell, Sudoku, and Solitaire? These are just a few of the multitude of focus games you can effortlessly get access to!

Meditation

Meditation is a daily activity that you can adopt and exploit in order to improve your focus. There are many meditational techniques to choose from and each one will impart a different benefit. Let us look at these techniques.

Breathing

Breathing meditation is quite popular and easy to perform. All you have to do is find yourself a quiet corner in the house and start inhaling and exhaling deeply. Focus on your breath and tune everything else out. Try to relax your mind and pay keen attention to how the air enters and exits your body. Don't breathe in through your mouth though, and breathe only through your nose. You can also do pranayama if you like, where you close one nostril and then exhale through the other. This is relatively easy to perform and involves holding your thumb over the nostril that you are not using. Remember when you breathe that it isn't just about breathing, it's about taking energy into your body, and that's what meditation is all about. When you speed-read after a meditation session, you will do so more attentively and understand more of what you are reading.

Walking

Walking meditation is a unique form of meditation. You must look for a large space where you can walk straight and just keep walking. Breathe in when you place your right leg forward and exhale when you place your left leg forward. Some people also like to walk around in circles. Concentrate on your breathing as you walk and try to forget about the rest of the world. This is a good form of meditation if you have a huge report to read and are dreading it. It clears your mind and makes you focus much better on your reading material, thus achieving more in a shorter period of time.

Mindfulness

Mindfulness is a technique that is meant to help you focus on just one thing at a time. It is obvious that there will be a million things on your mind on a daily basis and for this you need to focus on all the small things in the world. So right from washing your hands to cleaning the house, you need to remain mindful of each and every little activity. To stay focused on one thing is quite easy after a while. Think of nothing outside of the action that you are taking. If you are eating, concentrate on the tastes and textures that are put onto your tongue. Practicing mindfulness also makes your life more vibrant and alive.

These form different things that you can do to improve your focus and concentration to help speed-reading. Practice them and you are sure to see positive results in no time at all.

CHAPTER 10

THE 30-MINUTE RULE

When you wish to take up speed-reading, it is best that you make use of a minimum 30-minute daily practice schedule. Did you know that a daily practice routine of 30 minutes would improve your results significantly after a month? Try it and you'll be amazed; this doesn't merely apply to speed-reading, it relates to all other abilities you aspire to have in life.

Practice Reading Chapters

It is important to PRACTICE speed-reading at least a chapter at a time until you're comfortable with the process. Whether it is something from the newspaper or your email, quickly speed-read it. It is fine to read leisurely during the day, but there should be no cheating with your speed-reading practice. Use the techniques that were presented earlier, practice them, as they will help you read better and faster.

Practice Reading Entire Books

The next step is to speed-read entire books. It will seem impossible at the very beginning, but only practice makes perfect. Choose a small book for yourself that you can easily finish within a short period of time. Then move to a medium-sized book and then a big book. Make sure all the books are interesting, as a boring book will put you to sleep. Also, choose books that you are interested in because that will give you the initial concentration that you need to kick-start this habit.

Aiming High

Remember to aim high. If you can finish a 100-page book in 30 minutes, aim next for 200 pages within 30 minutes. You must aim high on a daily basis, and there should be nothing impossible for you. A very intelligent man once said that it's better to hit 60% of an immense goal than constantly hitting 100% of a trifling goal. Don't short yourself; think BIG and aim HIGH.

Remember that your reading can also be done from Kindle or through websites and that all of this helps your reading speed tremendously.

CHAPTER 11

FIXING YOUR CURRENT READING ISSUES

W hen you wish to take up speed-reading as a permanent choice, you must forget some of your old habits that might be pulling you down. In this chapter, we will look at how you can effectively break the shackles of your old habits.

Fixation

The fixation habit is one where you fixate your eyes over one or more of the words on the page. Remaining fixated over a single word for a long time can cause you to waste quite some time and it isn't effective toward reading either, so the idea is to break this habit once and for all.

Fixation is a natural human phenomenon that occurs with every individual. Right from a young age, we are forced to read a certain way, with emphasis on fixation. Consequently, it is probably the oldest reading habit that you possess, but the good news is it's fairly simple to break this habit and all you have to do is make use of your peripheral vision.

Human beings have something known as peripheral vision, as we discussed in a previous chapter. To illustrate this concept again, lift your head and look straight ahead. Without turning your eyes or your head, you can still look at whatever lies next to you, whether it be a wall or a television. This again is known as peripheral vision. You have to make use of this same vision to read more within a shorter period of time. When you utilize your peripheral vision, you can read more than a single word at a time. In fact, you can easily read two or three words and read at twice or thrice the speed.

It is a good idea to clump the words together as described in the technique chunk reading. This will ensure that you read faster and also understand whatever you read.

Practice daily and ensure that you do the right thing every time.

Regression

The next demon to tackle is known as regression. Regression is also known as re-reading. Now imagine seeing someone who is reading something. How many times do you see their eyes pass over a certain word but then come back to it? This is known as regression.

It is just as naturally occurring as fixation. You have to deal with it quickly if you wish to read quicker. Scientists have found that the average person spends about 20 minutes in an hour's worth of reading on regression. So it is important that you not waste so much time in a day.

Before you deal with it, let us look at some of the reasons why regression occurs. The main reason for regression to occur is a lack of focus. Your mind will be elsewhere while reading and this will cause you to re-read whatever that you already read; therefore, it is best that you remain fully focused during your readings. Don't keep thinking of other things, lest you end up wasting your time. Don't assume that your mind will automatically start to focus on the reading as soon as you pick the book up. You have to consciously make an effort to focus on the content when you wish to deal with regression.

The next common reason for the occurrence of regression is reading a unique word for the first time. You would not have heard of the word before and will wish to re-read it again to see if you actually do know the word. You will then spend a moment trying to remember such a word and waste time, so it is important to not do so. Once you come across such a word, remember the word and then look up its meaning later instead of trying to read it over and over again. If you make use of the Meta-Guiding technique, then you can make use of a pen and underline such a word, so that you will remember all the different words that you wish to look up.

The last reason for regression is going too fast. With speed-reading, it is quite common for people to lose control over their reading speeds. You might go so fast that you end up skipping a few lines in between. This can be a bad thing, as you will end up reading abruptly. So the best thing to do is garner control over your reading speed. Go slow at it and try not to skip anything in between; remember, we all must crawl before we can walk. Again, make use of the Meta-Guiding technique to help you.

Sub-vocalization

Sub-vocalization is the third roadblock. When you repeat the words in your head or say them out loud when you read something, your brain is forced to do two complex things at once. This can never be a good thing, and you must focus on only one activity at a time.

The best way to do so is by keeping your mouth closed while reading something and learning to chunk read. That way, you will not feel like reading anything vocally or internally. It sounds completely impossible, as you will be accustomed to reading it out loud, but do your best to not open your mouth at all. Concentrate on your reading alone and don't let your mind wander. You can chew on some gum if you prefer that.

When you wish to do away with your sub-vocalizing habit, you can make use of your vivid imagination. Your imagination will prevent you from reading out loud and you can also remember the things better.

These form the different old habits that you must deal with when you wish to improve your speed-reading.

CHAPTER 12

SPEED-READING MYTHS AND FAQS

Myths are an inevitable part of any topic and speed-reading also comes with its fair share of myths. It is our duty to debunk them and separate fact from fiction. Let us look at some of these myths in detail and debunk them.

Speed-reading is boring

The very first myth states that speed-reading is extremely boring; nonetheless, this theory should hold true only if you take the activity of reading in general as being boring. If you are already an avid reader who loves to read, then speed-reading will further enhance your experience, and if you are not such a keen reader, then speed-reading will help ignite a reading passion in you. Either way, you stand to gain from speed-reading. Yes, it will be a tough challenge at the very beginning, but nothing about it will be boring. In fact, it will be quite exciting and you will feel like speed-reading all the time.

Speed-reading is nothing but a gimmick

This is one doubt that many people have when it comes to speed-reading. They assume it is just a trick and does not really exist, but this is not true at all. Speed-reading is a real technique that is used to improve a person's reading skills. To supplement your belief, study and practice the techniques presented earlier then make a well-informed decision for yourself whether this is gimmick or a factual ability.

It will take too long to learn

This is just a bad myth. It will not take you a long time to learn speed-reading; in fact, don't worry about the time at all. Even if it takes you a couple of weeks or months, you will see steady, cumulative progress, and this will save you tons of time down the road. Don't wrongly assume that it will take you years together because the truth is, through consistent and persistent practice, you can undoubtedly cut your reading speed in half. Conversely, don't compare yourself to another person; perhaps they will read faster than you owing to their in-built capacity to learn faster, but don't be disheartened because hard work always pays off. You might learn slowly, but your habit will stick around longer. Spend each minute of speed-reading enjoying yourself and you will not even realize how and when your ability increases!

It is all about quick eyes

Not really. It is common to assume that it is necessary to move your eyes fast and run them over the words, but this is not really the case. Your eyes don't have to run for you to read fast; you need to maintain a consistent speed and not need to race. However, it will be to your advantage if you can run your eyes fast over the reading material, as it is an added benefit but it's definitely not compulsory. Accordingly, don't go all outlandish and merely move your eyes fast without looking at the words and not grasping anything.

Comprehension goes for a toss

It is quite normal to assume that you will not be able to comprehend when you speed-read and that your comprehension might go for a toss when you read really fast, but this is not true. You might actually grasp more when you speed-read because when you read the entire text within a short period of time, you will understand the topic better. Chunk reading, for example, requires your full attention and concentration, which will also help you grasp the topic better.

You need a guide at all times

Many people assume that you need a guide, like a finger or a scale to run under the sentence. This unquestionably helps, but if you are not accustomed to running your finger under the sentences then you don't have to do so. You can read without any such aid; nevertheless, when you do embark on your quest to read faster, it is recommended that you try Meta-Guiding at first until you get used to it.

Old habits die hard

This statement is not a myth but in relevance to speed-reading, it is. Don't assume that your old habits will keep pulling you down. They will be quite tough to get over, no doubt, but they can be easily fought off. All you need to be is determined and pay attention toward breaking your old habits for 21 days, and you'll be in the clear.

Speed-reading is best for fiction

This is not true. Speed-reading can be good for many types of texts. Right from fiction to non-fiction, you can use these techniques. As a matter of fact, there are certain techniques that are designed to help speed-read non-fiction books specifically! Don't think something is not speed-reading worthy. Once you take it up seriously, you will know how it is ideal for all types of books.

It is bad to not read wholly

This is another myth that bogs people down. They think that skimming and scanning will make them skip all the important parts of the text. The truth is, despite skipping paragraphs and sentences in between, you can still understand the gist of the topic, so don't think skimming and scanning are bad reading techniques.

The fault lies in me

Many people think that they are unable to read fast enough owing to their own visual limitations, but that has very little to do with your speed-reading skills. Don't think your eyes are the reason for your bad reading speeds. What's more probably instead is that your brain is not accustomed to reading so fast. It will take a little time for it to understand everything that you are expecting of it, so don't blame and go too hard on yourself; just trust in the system. If other people are able learn this, you absolutely can as well; it's not rocket science.

Using software is cheating

This is not true. You can make use of any software to help you read faster. Actually, you might end up learning faster after using the speed-reading software. Just make sure you are using a high-rated reliable course that helps you learn speed-reading at a faster pace.

Is speed-reading useful?

Yes. Speed-reading is extremely useful for everyone. There are several ways in which it will lessen the burden of going through large texts; you can easily finish a big book in no time at all. We looked at the different benefits of speed-reading in a previous chapter, and you will know why it is so important only after you take up speed-reading and achieve good speeds of reading and comprehension.

Is it for everyone?

Yes. All those who wish to read more in less time can take up this art. College students looking to excel in their academics can take up speed-reading. School students can use it to expand their comprehension on various subjects. It is also for professionals looking to improve their work knowledge. Housewives and senior citizens can also benefit tremendously. As you can see, there is no age limit to who can and who cannot use speed-reading. It is ideal that young children be introduced to it right from an early age, as they have ample time to read a broad curriculum and this would definitely be an advantage as they grow into adults.

Is it easy to learn?

Yes. Speed-reading is easy for people to learn. It will seem slightly difficult at the very beginning but, as you go on, it will become progressively easier. Try to take it up with an open mind and be prepared to push your boundaries; you will be surprised at your own abilities. There are some people who will learn the techniques swiftly, say in a week. So, you never know how quickly you might end up learning speed-reading. Take it up seriously and see it through, and you can thank me later.

Should I practice daily?

Yes. It is highly recommended that you practice daily, at least during the initial days. If you don't practice then your progress might be hindered. Try to read a wide range of books and texts and don't stick with the same old because it's good to familiarize yourself with how to speed-read from different angles. Nonetheless, don't start with a boring book. Set a specific time each day, say 30 minutes, and start from there. It may feel unusual at first doing the various techniques, but soon you'll get accustomed to it and appreciate what a dramatic difference this makes toward reading.

Can I have company?

Yes. You can choose a reading partner for yourself. The two of you can keep each other motivated, but of course don't force anyone and make sure they willingly wish to join in. You can ask your best friend to join in or a sibling. You can also ask a colleague to join you. You can join a speed-reading class if you like as well; this will allow you to have some inside tips on speed-reading and improve your chances of reading faster because it's always good learning with others.

Are there online tutorials?

Yes. There are online videos and classes that you can find online. You can look up the best one and join. In saying this, don't trust just any site; do your research and ensure that the one you choose is well-recognized. You might have to pay a little to take part in these courses, but they will be reasonably priced and well worth the value.

How to check my progress?

You must check your progress from time to time. Before starting out with the course, look at your speed while reading and make a note of it. Once you start with the course, make a note of your speed again. You should see a marked difference. Maintain a journal and fill in the details every day.

Is it useful for competitive exams?

Yes. It is an excellent way to prepare for competitive exams such as GRE and SATS. More than the studying, it will be ideal for revising the texts. You must try and use all the techniques like skimming and scanning instead of sticking to just one. There are testimonials of numerous people who claim to have excelled in competitive exams by making use of these same techniques.

Will I forget speed-reading?

No. It is highly improbable that you will forget how to speed-read. However, it is important that you practice often if you wish the habit to be ingrained into you; soon after doing this, it'll become a second nature to you and it'll change the way you read everything. Again, this all starts with practice, so pick a time and place and practice daily.

Is it a good technique for people with reading difficulties?

Yes. Speed-reading techniques are also ideal for those who have reading difficulties. Research has shown that some reading issues can be correlated to bad reading habits, which can definitely be improved upon through speed-reading techniques. In fact, speed-reading can be considered as good reading habits! You can cut a tree down with a hammer in perhaps 30 days, but with an axe you can cut down the same tree within perhaps 30 minutes; similarly with reading, you can digest a book with bad techniques in 30 days, but with good techniques you can probably do it in a lot less time!

These form the various questions that get asked on the topic and I hope you had yours answered efficiently.

CHAPTER 13

GENERIC TIPS FOR SPEED-READING

When it comes to speed-reading, there are simple things you should do to increase your interest in the subject and progress faster. In this chapter, we will look at a few fundamental things that you can do on a daily basis to increase your reading speed.

Timing

The very first thing to do is time your speed-reading. This means that you make use of a stopwatch to see how fast you can actually read. Once you start reading, start the clock and finish an entire page or chapter before hitting stop. Check the time and maintain a record of it. If you think your time is not impressive enough then you need to work on it further. Be wary not to cheat yourself of a learning opportunity here. You can also make use of a video recorder to see how your eyes are moving and whether you are actually making progress. Your aim should be to minimize the time taken to read each time and reduce it to the shortest possible time while maintaining a meaningful percentage of comprehension.

Schedule

Always maintain a set schedule when it comes to speed-reading. Work as per schedule and ensure that you always follow it. If you halt the habit even for one week, you will find it tough to take off from where you left; champions know that to develop a skill to its fullest, one most important things to do is to practice as much as possible. Do your best to not break the agenda. You can formulate a timetable that fits your needs. Ask your partner to help create it if you're bad at scheduling, as they will know when you are generally busy and when you are free. Once you formulate the timetable, create copies of it and keep one for yourself and also paste hard copies around you, in order to remain motivated.

Perfect Practice

They say that it's not practice that makes perfect, but perfect practice that makes perfect. Practice all the techniques every day to the best of your abilities. When practicing, remember to:

1. Read and understand the book through the table of contents

2. Ask questions regarding the book

3. Meta-Guiding

4. Visualization

5. Keyword search

6. Chunk read

7. Skimming

8. Scanning

Practice these every day and you'll increase your reading speed by 300% in no time!

Clean sheets

It is a golden rule to not mark your sheets with all sorts of color, as they will serve as distractions. Many people have the habit of using a highlighter as their Meta-Guiding tool and start highlighting all sorts of words and sentences. You must break this habit early if you wish to make steady progress with your speed-reading techniques. If you must highlight then use a light shaded pencil to underline certain words that are jargon or sentences that you do not understand. Once you finish reading, you can check the meanings of these.

Flexible

Remember that speed-reading does not always mean reading at breakneck speeds. You must have control over your reading and not go about it uncontrollably. You must ideally fluctuate between top speed and low speeds. Much like driving a motor vehicle, if the speed is getting too fast, then brake immediately, and reduce the speed by a little! So just by taking up speed-reading, it does not mean that you should forget about slow reading completely; you must allow it to remain in your memory and use it from time to time.

Distractions

Do not give in to distractions when you are speed-reading. Whether it is your cell phone or the television, it is best if everything were to be switched off when you wish to speed-read. You must also not have people around you talking, as that will distract you further. Try to cut down on all your distractions and you can make use of earplugs if you wish to concentrate on your text better. If you are expecting an urgent call then place the phone on vibrate mode and not ringer, as the ringing will distract you and throw your mind off of your reading mood.

Goals

Remember to always have only reasonable expectations out of your speed-reading adventures. If you go about it thinking you will turn into the best speed-reader in the world within a couple of days, then you had better drop the idea altogether! Speed-reading is like an amazing super power, no doubt, but you have to give yourself some time to develop the habit. Set yourself reasonable goals and go after them one after another. As soon as you attain a goal, tick it off and move to the next. However, your goals should be fulfilled within the said time frame.

Don't give up!

Giving up should never be an option for you. Don't give up on speed-reading no matter how tough it gets for you. Write down all your goals on a piece of paper and follow them through; it also helps to voice your goals to others. Announce to your family and friends that you are on a speed-reading mission and wish to improve your reading speed within a certain specified time. This will help you remain motivated and you will not feel like giving up on your speed-reading habits.

These form the several general tips on speed-reading that you can adopt to make it a smooth ride for yourself.

KEY TAKEAWAYS

The first thing to do is understand what speed-reading really is. As you know, all of us read a lot of things every single day. It imparts us knowledge and leaves us with information that is important for us to lead our daily lives and exploit our intelligence to the highest.

The troubling issue at hand is that we are unable to read enough, owing to living hectic lifestyles where we are split between work issues and family troubles. To solve this issue, we must undertake techniques that will allow us to read more within a short period of time and, for this, we can make use of speed-reading techniques.

By making use of these techniques, you can read a lot within a short period of time and it is not superficial reading; you will read thoroughly and have a complete understanding.

The average human brain is capable of reading 600 words a minute and we end up reading just 200, but this can be changed easily because all you have to do is understand and master a few different methods.

Several American presidents have advocated the use of speed-reading and encouraged several people to take it up and take advantage of it. By increasing your reading speed, you can easily read a lot more within a short period of time, leaving you with more time to do other things you value. Remember, time is money.

You must make use of concentration improvement techniques to improve your focus. Try to cut down on as many distractions as possible.

Create a set schedule to follow and stick to the timetable. Come up with something that is doable and flexible as opposed to a very strict schedule. You can take the help of a friend to create the schedule.

Remember to digest the table of contents and ask yourself a voluminous amount of questions concerning the book prior to even opening chapter 1. This will allow your mind to lock into exactly what you're reading, which will increase your reading speed tremendously. Also, as you're reading, practice visualizing images in your head; it's been said that a picture is worth a thousand words!

Don't let your confidence delude you. Understand that there are words that you have yet to learn, so keyword search them to understand the meanings before you embark.

Another speed-reading technique is known as skimming. Skimming refers to going through bits and pieces of the text to understand the gist of it. You can read the entire book using this technique or use it as a precursor to your regular reading techniques.

The scanning technique is the next method to choose. Scanning allows you to look for specific bits and pieces of information in the text such as names, numbers, and central ideas.

The next technique to adopt is known as Meta-Guiding. With Meta-Guiding, you can make use of a pacer or a guide that you will run under the words and sentences. You can use your finger or a ruler or even a thread. As long as it guides your vision, you can make use of it.

Remember to take advantage of online resources. You can easily learn to speed-read by making use of speed-reading software, but you must look for the best and most efficient one.

When you start speed-reading, you need to break some of your old habits. Some of these old habits include fixation, regression, and sub-vocalization. Effectively eliminating all of these will help you better your reading skills.

There is a certain lifestyle that you need to take up when you wish to speed-read with ease. These include eating brain-healthy foods and not consuming those that are bad for your health, sleeping enough, etc. All these will go a long way in helping you improve your speed-reading skills and your health in general.

You need to take up speed-reading as a lifestyle choice and not a mere fancy activity that you wish to abandon within a couple of days. Maintain a daily record of your progress and you will know how useful it really is to speed-read something.

CONCLUSION

Congratulations! You have come to the end of this book. We covered much material on how to increase your reading speed and comprehension by as much as 300%. In Chapter 1, you learned the basics of speed-reading, including the importance of speed-reading, the common obstacles to reading faster, and the importance of understanding the things you read for comprehension. In Chapter 2, you read about how to prepare well for your speed-reading sessions, including assessing your words-per-minute (reading speed) and effective-words-per-minute (comprehension). In Chapters 3 to 4, you learned key speed-reading and comprehension techniques and exercises to help you master the techniques even more. Next, you learned how to maximize the benefits of the techniques and exercises you learned by supplementing them with non-reading approaches like the optimal reading environment, improving focus, eating the right foods, exercising, getting enough quality sleep, and MORE.

What's next? It's been said that knowing is just half the battle. The other half is applying that knowledge. That being said, I highly encourage you to start applying the techniques and doing the exercises, to help you master the techniques even better, consistently for the next few weeks. Note that increasing your reading speed and comprehension by up to 300% doesn't normally happen overnight but, as with most disciplines, consistency, patience, and perseverance will help you do that. Stick with the exercises and you'll see the results in a few weeks.

Here's to your speed-reading success! Cheers!

FREE BONUS

Thanks for being a loyal reader. I hope you have found this book to be beneficial and helpful to the personal mastery of your life. As a reward, here is a FREE bonus guide (Worth over $30) that can help you accomplish your goals in life no matter what they may be.

Please type the below URL into your web browser
to receive the FREE BONUS

https://amazing-funnels.leadpages.co/personal-mastery-bonus/

Made in the USA
Lexington, KY
30 May 2017